GOD BREATHES ON BLENDED FAMILIES WORKBOOK
Copyright© 2002 by Moe Becnel/ Paige Becnel

All rights reserved, including the right to reproduce this book or portions thereof in any form whatsoever, without the written permission of the Authors.

Library of Congress Cataloging-in-Publication Data

ISBN: 0-9678680-1-7

Published by Healing Place Productions
19202 Highland Road
Baton Rouge, Louisiana 70809
1-225-753-2273

Cover design by Jimmy Cook, Baton Rouge, LA

Drama Scripts by Shanna Forrestall, Arts Ministry Leader
  (See Appendix C)   Healing Place Church, Baton Rouge, LA

Moe and Paige Becnel are founders of BLENDING A FAMILY MINISTRY, dedicated to helping blended families achieve greatness.

Visit our website at   www.blendingAfamily.com

Printed in the United States of America

BLENDING A FAMILY MINISTRY

Moe & Paige Becnel founded BLENDING A FAMILY MINISTRY to be a resource for stepfamilies who desire God's Plan and God's Best for their families. Our goal is to help stepfamilies become real loving families and to see these families *thrive*, not just survive. The desired result is that the cycle of divorce will be broken in people's lives.

Blending A Family Ministry Mission Statement

The mission of Blending A Family Ministry is to be a healing place,
to be a source of help for today's remarried families,
to give guidance concerning the issues that blended families face,
to help remarried couples and their children to become the very best family that God intended,
to dismiss the thought that blended families are second class families,
and to see thousands of blended families flourish as they develop into the loving,
peace-filled safe-haven that God intended the home to be.

Moe & Paige's first book, GOD BREATHES ON BLENDED FAMILIES, was written in hopes of helping all blended families to become true loving families. The blended family needs to provide a solid foundation for their children, established through God's love, mercy and grace. The book has been a great source of hope, encouragement and advice, as people see that what the Becnel's experienced in their family is very similar to what many other blended families face. God has truly blessed this work, as He is using it to help other families get the victory. Many positive comments have been received from families that have read their book.
GOD BREATHES ON BLENDED FAMILIES is recommended reading for stepfamilies by www.vieuxpoint.com (an online magazine), www.iStepfamily.com (an online stepfamily website), and by Debra Maffett, Host, Harvest TV.

GOD BREATHES ON BLENDED FAMILIES WORKBOOK, was written in 2002 to assist couples in becoming successful blended families by applying God's principles to their families.

Become a <u>BLENDING A FAMILY</u> Support Group Leader in your church or community!!!

Call, email, or write us for more information!

Visit our Website at <u>www.blendingAfamily.com</u>

About the Authors

Currently, Moe & Paige Becnel are the Singles Pastors at Healing Place Church in Baton Rouge, Louisiana, serving under Sr. Pastors Dino & DeLynn Rizzo. They lead the vibrant singles/ single again ministry entitled TGIS (Thank God I'm Single). Visit the Singles Ministry site at www.healingplacechurch.org. They have also written parts of, and teach Healing Place Church's REACH FOR RECOVERY, a divorce recovery program.

Moe & Paige have hearts to establish singles/ single again ministries in churches across America, to be a healing place for those who have experienced divorce or death of a spouse, as well as for those living the role of single parents. Many single people need recovery from divorce or other broken relationships, true friends, and a continual challenge to lead productive and satisfying lives in their singleness.

The Becnels founded BLENDING A FAMILY MINISTRY. The goal of BLENDING A FAMILY MINISTRY is to help remarried families become a true family -- abounding in love, respect, acceptance and grace. It is time for the Cycle-of-Divorce to be broken in people's lives!

The Becnels wrote GOD BREATHES ON BLENDED FAMILIES, and GOD BREATHES ON BLENDED FAMILIES WORKBOOK in hopes of helping thousands of blended families to become a true loving family that provide a solid foundation for their children, established through God's love, mercy and grace.

Moe & Paige Becnel are natives of New Orleans, LA and have resided in Baton Rouge, LA since 1994. They met in a Christian singles ministry in 1987 and were married in 1989, blending a family of 5 children. They have taught several Bible studies over the years and have been involved in missions in Africa, Honduras, Costa Rica and Peru.

To date, they have appeared and discussed their book on the Sierra Show on TBN, Harvest TV on LeSea Broadcasting and The Ed Buggs radio talk show in Baton Rouge. They have written articles on blended families for the New Orleans *The Times Picayune*, Baton Rouge *In-Register* magazine and *City Social* magazine. They also write columns for www.vieuxpoint.com on-line magazine, and www.iStepfamily.com on-line stepfamily magazine.

The Becnels have spoken at family conferences, family seminars and singles conferences.

The Becnels are available to speak and assist families:
- ➢ Marriage seminars & conferences
- ➢ Blended family classes & discussion groups
- ➢ Blended family seminars
- ➢ Singles Conferences

CONTACT THE AUTHORS

Email: blendingAfamily@cox.net
Or: paige.becnel@healingplacechurch.org

For speaking engagements:
Call Healing Place Church at 1-225-753-2273

ORDER FORM

To order more Books and Workbooks for friends, neighbors, or co-workers:

GOD BREATHES ON BLENDED FAMILIES
     ISBN: 0-9678680-0-9   Retail: $9.00 X Quantity_____   = Total_____

GOD BREATHES ON BLENDED FAMILIES WORKBOOK
     ISBN: 0-9678680-1-7   Retail: $12.95 X Quantity_____   = Total_____

Please complete this order form and mail to:
     Healing Place Church
     19202 Highland Road   or call HPC at 1-225-753-2273
     Baton Rouge, LA 70809   or order on-line at www.healingplacechurch.org/products

START YOUR OWN BLENDING A FAMILY SUPPORT GROUP!

CALL FOR QUANTITY DISCOUNTS!

ORDER FORM

To order more Books and Workbooks for friends, neighbors, or co-workers:

GOD BREATHES ON BLENDED FAMILIES
     ISBN: 0-9678680-0-9   Retail: $9.00 X Quantity_____   = Total_____

GOD BREATHES ON BLENDED FAMILIES WORKBOOK
     ISBN: 0-9678680-1-7   Retail: $12.95 X Quantity_____   = Total_____

Please complete this order form and mail to:
     Healing Place Church   or call HPC at 1-225-753-2273
     19202 Highland Road
     Baton Rouge, LA 70809   or order on-line at www.healingplacechurch.org/products

START YOUR OWN BLENDING A FAMILY SUPPORT GROUP!

CALL FOR QUANTITY DISCOUNTS!

Dedicated with all our love to all of our children

Melanie Becnel Broga
Jonathan Broga
Nicole Morriz Duplechain
Brad Duplechain
Jordan Becnel
Kristen Morriz
Jessica Becnel

Table of Contents

Definitions
Session 1   Introduction
Session 2   God's Plan for Blended Families
Session 3   Two Must Become One
Session 4   Divisions Within Families
Session 5   Ingredients for Healthy Blended Families
Session 6   The Children's Perspective
Session 7   Responsibilities of a Stepparent
Session 8   Interference from Extended Family
Session 9   Vision and Purpose/ Prayer– An Awesome Thing
Appendix A   Scripture References
Appendix B   Resolving Conflicts in Life
Appendix C   Suggested Drama Scripts

Scripture taken from the HOLY BIBLE, NEW INTERNATIONAL VERSION (R), NIV(R)
Copyright(c) 1973, 1978, 1984 by Zondervan Publishing House.
All Rights Reserved.

Definitions

Blended Family - Any marriage in which at least one of the spouses becomes a new parent, regardless of the age of the children.

Blended --- to mix together, so that the things mixed cannot be separated or individually distinguished
         --- to mix together, especially in such a way as to form one product

Natural parent --- the maternal or paternal biological parent

Natural child or children --- your biological child or children

New parent --- the spouse who *gains* a child or children through marriage

New child or children --- child or children *gained* through marriage; your stepchildren; your spouse's natural child or children

Extended parents --- parents of both spouses

Extended family --- parents, brothers, sisters, grandparents, aunts, uncles and friends of both spouses

Former spouse --- more commonly referred to as ex-spouse, or "x"

GOD BREATHES ON BLENDED FAMILIES WORKBOOK

Session 1

Registration (Name, Address, Phone, Email)

Opener

Tell about your family:
1. How long have you been married?_____
2. How did you meet?_____
3. How many children, their names and ages?_____
   _____
4. What is your expectation from this group?_____
   _____

SCRIPTURES CAN BE FOUND IN APPENDIX "A", OR IN THE BOOK.

Introduction

As we have met with several blended families who have read GOD BREATHES ON BLENDED FAMILIES, we have often seen that these families grasp the ideas established in the book, but still struggle to make the necessary changes in their own family. GOD BREATHES ON BLENDED FAMILIES WORKBOOK is written to assist blended families in reaching the full potential of being the loving family unit that God designed a family to be, in which <u>every family member</u> is an integral part, feels truly loved and is of equal importance.

As you and your spouse proceed through GOD BREATHES ON BLENDED FAMILIES WORKBOOK, it is of utmost importance to understand and believe that:
1. <u>Time alone does not cause your family to blend.</u>
   A psychologist stated that it takes a blended family an average of 4 to 8 years to "gel", and finally feel like a real family.
   However, do not think you can just wait a certain number of years, and it will take care of itself. Sticking your head in the sand and doing nothing, or refusing to change will only make things worse.
   Blending a family takes commitment, patience, endurance and a "never quit attitude"!

2. <u>God is in you, and is on your side.</u> God wants your new family to be made complete, according to His design for families. By His Holy Spirit, God will show you the solutions to make your family a success, and will help you to make the changes that YOU need to make.
   Write down the highlights of what these passages mean to you:
   Psalm 28:7_____

Psalm 34:18_____

Isaiah 42:16_____

John 14: 26_____

Romans 8: 34 _____

3. <u>The successful blending of your family is a team effort.</u> Do not expect your spouse to carry the ball or make all the changes. You both share the goal and the responsibility for success. (You can change no one.)
Write down the highlights of what these passages mean to you:
Mark 10: 6-9_____

_____

Ecclesiastes 4: 9-10._____

_____

4. <u>Prayer is of utmost importance</u> in your walk through GOD BREATHES ON BLENDED FAMILIES WORKBOOK together. The examples in GOD BREATHES ON BLENDED FAMILIES may not specifically address the answers to the particular circumstances or personalities in your family, but God has the answers, and He will reveal the answers to you in your prayer time with Him.

Oil in the Engine
The best way to describe the effect of prayer on your family is the same effect that motor oil has in an automobile engine. Without oil, the engine quickly overheats due to friction. Friction will destroy the engine. With proper oil levels in the engine, the engine friction is minimized and the engine will operate properly and last a very long time. <u>Consider prayer the oil that you apply to your family to keep parts and situations from overheating and damaging the family relationships and environment.</u> Prayer over every person and every situation in your family will cause it to operate according to God's design.

<u>Write down the highlights of what these passages mean to you:</u>
2 Chronicles 20: 12-15_____

_____

1 Chronicles 5: 20_____

_____

Philippians 4: 6-7_____

_____

5. <u>It is necessary for you and your children to avoid another divorce</u> --- AT ALL COST!
> Your new family needs to become your children's role model of a loving home.
> Your children need to experience true love, nurturing, security and stability in your home. Thus far, your children have only known broken relationships that they did not initiate.
> They now need to see your family thrive --- not just survive!
> It is the role of the parents to set the tone, attitude and atmosphere in the home. (If allowed, the children will often take on this role.)
DEVELOP A WINNING – NEVER QUITTING – ATTITUDE!

HOMEWORK:

1. Read ***Restoration After Divorce*** (GOD BREATHES ON BLENDED FAMILIES pages 6-8)
   FAILURE → REPENTANCE → FORGIVEN → REDEMPTION → RESTORATION

2. If you have experienced divorce, answer the following questions:

   a.) Do you blame God for your divorce or other failure in your past?_____
   Blaming God causes bitterness in our heart. God is good, loving and caring!

   b.) Have you searched your heart to identify things that you may have done in your previous marriage that added to the deterioration of that relationship? If not, do it now! Write down what you have identified:_____
   _____
   _____

   c.) What actions have you taken to change yourself?_____
   _____
   _____
   _____

   d.) Have you repented for the hurt that you may have caused in your former spouse and previous marriage?_____

   e.) Have you forgiven your former spouse and all those involved for the hurt they may have caused you?_____

   f.) Do you know and believe that God desires to restore you, and make your new family a real, loving family?_____

3. Review the following scriptures and write down the key points:
   1 John 1: 9 _____
   _____
   Psalm 103: 12 _____
   _____
   Psalm 103: 4-8_____
   _____
   John 10: 10 _____
   _____
   1 Corinthians 13: 4-6 _____
   _____

4. Spend time in prayer thanking God for His forgiveness, His mercy, His grace and the brand new life He has for you. Ask God to forgive you for any wrong attitudes and unforgiveness that you have identified.

5. Read Chapter 1 of GOD BREATHES ON BLENDED FAMILIES for next week.

GOD BREATHES ON BLENDED FAMILIES WORKBOOK

Session 2

Opener

Each couple gets 10 blocks. The husband guides his wife in placing the blocks to build the vision in his mind. The wife only listens and follows instructions – she cannot speak. Time limit is 3 minutes.   (Now reverse roles, and repeat exercise.)

1. What did you feel when you were giving instructions?
    HUSBAND_____

    WIFE_____

2. What did you feel when you were receiving instructions and could not ask questions?
    HUSBAND_____

    WIFE_____

3. Did you think you gave better instructions than your spouse?
    HUSBAND_____WIFE_____

4. What emotions surfaced during the exercise?
    _____   _____   _____   _____   _____   _____

DISCUSSION OF PRIDE
- Definition of Pride = justifiable self-respect; superiority; arrogance
- The middle letter of pride is "i". Pride is about the "i" in us. It looks to self without regard to other's feelings, needs or desires.
- Pride's self-seeking ways serve only to damage relationships around us, and stops successful relationships in our lives.
- Pride causes your partner or children to feel inferior, insignificant, unappreciated, and worthless.
- Symptoms of pride: > what is in it for me   > wanting your way, or no way
            > your opinions are always right > sarcasm or criticism, followed by "I was only joking."

Discuss Proverbs 13:10_____

_____

Read and discuss the following passages in which pride destroyed families:
        Genesis 21: 8-14 (Story of Abraham, Sarah, Hagar & Ishmael)
        Genesis Chapter 27 (Story of Jacob and Esau) - NOT IN APPENDIX A
Opinions: Our opinions are not always right, and other's opinions are not always wrong. Opinions are partially based on facts, but are also based on individual personality, personal preferences, backgrounds, education, family history, religious beliefs, etc. The problem with opinions is <u>not</u> that everyone has one, <u>but</u> that each person thinks theirs is right.   Consider other's opinions for a change. God made us all different on purpose --- by His design. We need to respect His idea.

Discuss previous homework assignment.

Chapter 1   God's Plan for Blended Families

I.   *Struggles of Blended Families*
GOD BREATHES ON BLENDED FAMILIES pages 9-12

Do you and your spouse have different ideas and ways of seeing things?
HUSBAND _____ WIFE _____
Are you struggling with the same issues over and over again?
WIFE _____ HUSBAND _____
Does the slow process of your family blending frustrate you?
HUSBAND _____ WIFE _____
Are there different rules and different styles of discipline in your family?
WIFE _____ HUSBAND _____

List your marriage's/ family's top three struggles:
HUSBAND
1. _____
_____
2. _____
_____
3. _____
_____

WIFE
1. _____
_____
2. _____
_____
3. _____
_____

II.   *God's Knowledge of Blended Families*
GOD BREATHES ON BLENDED FAMILIES pages 12-13

Read Jeremiah 1: 5.
Did God know you at birth?_____ 10 years ago?_____
     Last year?_____
Does God know you today?_____
Does God already know you 10 years from now?_____

Read Jeremiah 29: 11.
Did God have a plan for you when you were born?_____
     10 years ago?_____ Last year?_____
Does God already have a plan for you 10 years from now?_____

III. *God Has A Plan/ God's Timing*
GOD BREATHES ON BLENDED FAMILIES pages 13-18

Read the story of creation in Genesis Chapter 1.

God took His time.
If creating something took God time, it will take time for you and your spouse to create a new, loving family! *Even though it took longer than we had hoped, God was always - and still is - in control.*
How much time have the people in your new family had to bond?_____

Before God performed any creation of life, God took time to prepare the earth.
He spent 4 days separating things. He then created all living creatures in 2 days.
The Holy Spirit "hovered." Hover means to brood over, to cherish.

What 4 things did God need to separate to prepare the earth and heavens for His living creatures?
1._____
2._____
3._____
4._____

Separation must take place before orderly creation can begin.

Here are some areas God had to do some separating in the Becnels --- before He could create LIFE in our family:

Our thoughts = Of why, of doubt, of "flawed human reasoning"   Read Isaiah 55: 9
Our thoughts can so often get in the way of what God is trying to do for us.
Our negative thoughts and flawed human reasoning are like muddy shoes, trampling all over the work God is trying to do.

Our pride = wanting to be in control; not letting go of "our way"; taking from the other.
Pride only serves to separate, hurt and destroy.
Humble people have a heart for others.

Our past --- failures; hurts; disappointments; broken dreams. These are not stumbling blocks to God!
Unload your bags of guilt, sin, failure, bitterness, criticism, and blame.
Travel light.
Look forward, not backward.

Our ignorance of God's Plan
God has principles in His Word for our life, and family.
We can have an encounter with Jesus, the Prince of Peace, but we also need to understand and apply God's principles to develop love and peace in our home.

Define the areas in you that God needs to do some separating. (See the categories below to help you focus on areas in your life.)

Be honest with yourself! Be honest with your spouse!

>> *Exclude discussing the children in this exercise.*

(You do not need to have all the answers now; the book further discusses areas that hinder family unity.)

Write down what you have identified:

HUSBAND

Your Darkness (sin) from His Light? _____

Your Pride from His Humility? _____

Your human reasoning from His Principles? _____

Your Past from His future for you? _____

Your Selfishness from His Self-less Love? _____

WIFE

Your Darkness (sin) from His Light? _____

Your Pride from His Humility? _____

Your human reasoning from His Principles? _____

Your Past from His future for you? _____

Your Selfishness from His Self-less Love? _____

HOMEWORK:

Begin this assignment by praying together with your spouse.

1. Continue from above in discussing the things within each of you that need to be separated before God can begin creating you and your children into a new family. *Continue to write down what you have identified in the above spaces.*

2. Together with your spouse, pray the prayer on page 19 of the book. Pray for each other, and for every family member.

3. Read Chapter 2 of GOD BREATHES ON BLENDED FAMILIES for next week.

GOD BREATHES ON BLENDED FAMILIES WORKBOOK

Session 3

Opener

Act out or discuss this situation:

A couple has been married for 1 year, and they find themselves pressured into eating lunch every Sunday with his or her parents. Both parents get flustered each time they attempt to make their own plans for Sunday afternoon.

The couple is frustrated with the situation, but neither wants to hurt their parents' feelings. So they live with the situation that their parents "expect" them to have Sunday lunch with them every other week. The pressure begins to wear on the couple's relationship, and they begin to take it out on each other, putting their in-laws down.

1. Does anyone here live in, or know of a similar situation?_____

2. What should the couple do?_____

_____

3. What are some practical solutions?_____

_____

_____

Review previous homework assignment.

Chapter 2　　　　　Two Must Become One

I.　*God's Principles for Marriage*
　　　　　GOD BREATHES ON BLENDED FAMILIES pages 20-24

Read Genesis 2: 22-24.

VOWS at your wedding --- "OK, we are now one!" --- NO.

VOWS are your commitment to each other to work to become one, and to never quit. It is a process!

List the three key instructions found in Gen. 2: 22-24 for a successful marriage.

1._____

_____

2._____

_____

3._____

_____

Leaving father and mother
Your spouse must become more important than all other relationships!
Are we to break off all other relationships?
Two cannot become one if other people are involved in the decisions.

(Have your extended family members put expectations on you?)

United to his wife
Definition of "unite" – see GOD BREATHES ON BLENDED FAMILIES pg. 23
Make a two-handed covenant with your spouse.
"Your spouse must take the highest place of honor, respect, and admiration in your life, excepting ONLY to your relationship with God!"

Two shall become one (in body, mind, and spirit)
Prior to marriage you were two people, and likely had different goals, beliefs, ideas, agendas, & interests.
Read and discuss Philippians 2: 1-2_____
Becoming one includes being in one mind and setting common goals.

II.   *The Bride of Jesus Christ*
GOD BREATHES ON BLENDED FAMILIES pages 25-28

Read and discuss the questions on pages 25-26 of the BOOK with your spouse or group to gain understanding of how God sees you and how important you are to God. Write down any thoughts you have through this:

Does God LOVE You? John 3:16_____
_____
_____

Does God HONOR You? Galatians 3: 26_____
_____
_____

Does God RESPECT You? Matthew 28: 18-20_____
_____
_____

Does God ADMIRE You? Genesis 1: 27; Romans 8: 29; Jeremiah 29: 11_____
_____
_____

Does God NEED You? Mark 16: 15-18_____
_____
_____

Does God WANT You? Deuteronomy 14: 2; 2 Corinthians 6: 18; John 15: 15_____

_____

_____

Read Ephesians 5: 25
Husbands and wives are to have the same relationship with each other that Christ and His church have.
The strongest love relationship is based on mutual love, mutual honor, mutual respect, mutual admiration, mutual need and mutual want!
People who enter into a marriage for the purposes of improving finances, filling the void of loneliness, having someone to cook and clean for them, or meeting their other needs usually wind up with a strained relationship.

God must still be your source! Your spouse is not designed to fulfill that role!
"God must be your source, your provider and your strength. Only then will you serve your spouse, rather than expecting to be served."

IN THE HEAT OF BATTLE
We often hurt the very one we VOWED to become one with.
Sarcasm (definition – 'sarcasmo') – Tear flesh, like a wolf devours its prey.

Damaged relationships are not quickly or easily restored.

Fight right! Fight your adversary!
1. Ephesians 6: 12   We wrestle not against flesh and blood
2. Slow to speak = SHUT UP
3. Calm down first.
4. Communicate, compromise, and work it out.
5. Remember, you both have (or should have) the same goals.
6. Pick your battles. Some things are not worth an argument. (Get rid of "pet peeves".)

JESUS NEVER TEARS HIS BRIDE DOWN!

In your opinion, what key area does your marriage need the most growth?
HUSBAND

_____

_____

WIFE

_____

_____

What changes do you perceive that <u>you</u> need to make to achieve this growth?
WIFE

_____

_____

HUSBAND

_____

_____

III. Appreciating Your Spouse

God made your spouse unique, with certain gifts, talents and abilities.
List some unique qualities of your spouse:
YOUR HUSBAND
Uniqueness _____
Gifts _____
Talents _____
Abilities _____
YOUR WIFE
Uniqueness _____
Gifts _____
Talents _____
Abilities _____

Is your spouse your best friend?
The MAIN person I want to live the rest of my life with is MY BEST FRIEND!

Test to see if you consider your spouse your best friend – answer the following:
    If you have something good or bad happen, who do you go to first?
        Your spouse? Your Mom or Dad? Your child? Another friend? Your former
        spouse?

If your spouse is not your best friend, you need to develop that relationship.

A BEST FRIEND helps and serves their friend.

As you enlarge your appreciation for your spouse, their gifts and their dreams, you will become their BEST FRIEND!

Read the bulleted thoughts about your spouse on page 28 of GOD BREATHES ON BLENDED FAMILIES.

The ULTIMATE MARRIAGE is one in which each spouse is assisting the other to accomplish their goals.

HOMEWORK:

1. Do you know what your spouse's goals, ambitions, desires and dreams are? If not, ask them. Write them down here:
   YOUR WIFE
   Goals _____
   Ambitions _____
   Desires _____
   Dreams _____
   YOUR HUSBAND
   Goals _____
   Ambitions _____
   Desires _____
   Dreams _____

2. Pray together and lift up your spouse, and their ambitions, goals and dreams. Pray for your marriage, your oneness and your new family.

3. Go on a "different" date with your spouse. Try something new, like bungee jumping together! Enjoy each other on a long weekend away.

4. Spend time together finding out your spouse's dreams, hopes, and personal interests. Discuss your future together.

5. Edify your spouse! Tell them how much they mean to you, and how they add value to your life (HUSBANDS – THINK BEFORE YOU SPEAK!)

6. Read Chapter 3 of GOD BREATHES ON BLENDED FAMILIES for next week.

GOD BREATHES ON BLENDED FAMILIES WORKBOOK

Session 4

Opener (See Appendix C – Drama 1)

Act out or discuss this scene
A stepmother is concerned about her "new" 5-year-old son riding his bike in the street. Dad is unconcerned – thinks his son is responsible enough. His reaction becomes a heated discussion between them. The stepmother is made to feel that her maternal instincts are not important in this family, and that her opinion does not matter.
They decide to sit and work together on mutual guidelines for "their son". They begin to write out a new set of rules acceptable to both spouses.

Points from the situation:
1. Two sets of rules
2. Two opinions: one thing about opinions --- everyone has one
3. Both could have valid opinions and good reasons
4. Sounds like an argument – agitation – Why?
5. Good solution?

Working together, being willing to see each other's viewpoint, and writing down a workable solution is a step to becoming one in mind.

Review previous homework assignment.

Chapter 3   Divisions Within Families
GOD BREATHES ON BLENDED FAMILIES pages 29-47

I.   Vision for Your New Family

Write down the vision and purpose you each have for your new family:
HUSBAND

_____
_____
_____
_____

WIFE

_____
_____
_____
_____

II. You have an adversary!

And it is not your spouse - or your stepchildren! It is not even your former spouse!
1 Peter 5: 8 reads, *"Be sober, be vigilant; because your adversary the devil walks about like a roaring lion, seeking whom he may devour."*

Ephesians 6: 12 says, *"For we do not wrestle against flesh and blood, but against principalities, against powers, against the rulers of the darkness of this age, against spiritual hosts of wickedness in the heavenly places."*

HOW TO GET ON THE OFFENSIVE, FIGHTING FOR YOUR FAMILY:
(GOD BREATHES ON BLENDED FAMILIES page 30)
1. Applying God's Principles
   Read Psalm 127: 1_____

2. Developing the Character of Christ in yourself. (Galatians 5: 22)

LOVE	PATIENCE	FAITHFULNESS
JOY	KINDNESS	GENTLENESS
PEACE	GOODNESS	SELF-CONTROL

III. Divisions Within Families
GOD BREATHES ON BLENDED FAMILIES pages 31-34

Matthew 12: 25b "...every city or household divided against itself will not stand."
Divisions are Satan's strategy.
Divisions creep in subtly --- you may not be aware of them.
Divisions have the same effect as erosion.

Signs of division --- Review GOD BREATHES ON BLENDED FAMILIES page 32-33

Exercise: Prepare a basket with several household items, such as pepper shaker, bandaids, small towel, soap, fork, candle, apple, pear, toothpick, small funnel, etc. Pass the basket to each husband and wife and ask them to take an item that best describes their feelings today about their blended family.

Write down the item you chose, and describe how that item represents your feeling regarding any issues that you and your spouse are dealing with in your home:
HUSBAND

_____

_____

WIFE

_____

_____

Spouse – there is a reason your spouse is feeling this way!

Let's try to identify some divisions in your family. Ponder the following questions:
>What do you disagree about?
>What do you argue about?
>Is there friction between family members?
>What would you like to see changed in your family?

Each of you write down the three most dominant divisions that you perceive in your new home: (It is OK if your answers do not match.)

WIFE

1._____

2._____

3._____

HUSBAND

1._____

2._____

3._____

If you have identified some divisions, DO NOT FEEL DEFEATED! It is important that together you identified the key divisions within your family.
If you did not already, acknowledge how your spouse is feeling!

IV. *Finding Solutions that Work*
>GOD BREATHES ON BLENDED FAMILIES pages 34–47

Review each of the items below (found on pages 34–47), and the advice under each subject. Write down any useful advice that you found for the divisions within your family that you previously listed:

a. Respect for the New Parent_____
_____
_____

Manipulation occurs in all homes, but in blended families the child often challenges or attacks the new parent.

b. "Step" Syndrome_____
_____
_____

c. "Your" vs. "My" Children_____
_____
_____

d. Discipline_____

_____

_____

e. Submission After Independence_____

_____

_____

f. Favoritism = Double Standards_____

_____

_____

There is nothing that will create disunity in the home quicker than favoritism.

      In Genesis 37: 3-4, we read the story of Joseph and his brothers. It reads,
"Now Israel loved Joseph more than all his children, because he was the son of his old age. Also he made him a tunic of many colors. But when his brothers saw that their father loved him more than all his brothers, they hated him and could not speak peaceably to him."

Yet, favoritism in a blended family can be even more pronounced because people tend to love their natural child more than a child that was not born to them. Any new children born of the spouses tend to get more attention than the stepchildren do in the home.

Every spouse and every child needs to feel accepted by the other family members.

For your family to truly blend, this obstacle must be overcome!

Time and effort are required.

(This issue is further discussed in a later chapter.)

g. Child Wants Natural Parents Back Together _____

_____

_____

Almost every child of divorce has a DREAM to see their natural parents back together, *even after one or both are remarried! And they may hold on to that dream for years. "The Parent Trap" movies are more than cute --- they are reality!!!*

h. Child Wants to Live with Other Natural Parent_____

_____

_____

    1) Child misses other parent

    2) Child may not accept or feel accepted by stepparent.

        If you are the new parent and there is tension between you and your new child, you must take action. If that child goes to live with the other natural parent because of tension or rejection from you, your spouse will resent you.

i. Your Spouse's Need for Security_____

_____

_____

    Intimidated by your relationship with former spouse.

    Making your house your spouse's home.

    Extended family issues.

V. Back to Your Vision and Purpose

At the beginning of this Session, each of you wrote the Vision and Purpose you have for your new family. Based on any divisions that you identified, you need to develop a strategy to overcome and remove the divisions, and the positive steps you need to make to accomplish your vision.

Write your Strategy to Remove Divisions and Accomplish your Vision & Purpose:

_____
_____
_____
_____
_____
_____

God has a vision for your family, too! He wants love and grace to flow freely in your home. He wants all members to accept, respect and embrace each other!

Do not be overwhelmed with the task before you. You, your spouse and God are more than enough to achieve greatness in your family!

> Psalm 37: 4-5 says, "Delight yourself also in the LORD, and He shall give you the desires of your heart. Commit your way to the LORD, Trust also in Him, and He shall bring it to pass."

HOMEWORK:

1. Review the divisions you identified. Are there any others that you missed earlier.

2. Pray together, lifting up your spouse and your family needs.
   Pray over the divisions you identified.

3. Prayerfully work out a strategy to address and eliminate any identified divisions. Write it down! In prayer, ask God to show you how to handle each issue and each personality in your home.

4. Plan a family day or night together. Be sure all family members are there.
   (At the least, set a date to have your family day.)

5. Read Chapter 4 of GOD BREATHES ON BLENDED FAMILIES for next week.

GOD BREATHES ON BLENDED FAMILIES WORKBOOK

Session 5

Opener

Say something positive about your spouse in one or more of these areas!

Attributes_____	Talents_____
Their heart_____	Abilities_____
Something good they did_____	A Good Habit_____

Review previous homework assignment.

Chapter 4　　Ingredients for Healthy Blended Families
GOD BREATHES ON BLENDED FAMILIES pages 48-55

I.　Individual Wholeness
GOD BREATHES ON BLENDED FAMILIES pages 48-49

Individual wholeness is being secure as an individual – knowing and liking who you are. It is also knowing who God is, and who God wants to be to you.

To be a successful marriage partner, it is vital that you do not carry your past or any unforgiveness, resentment or bitterness into your new marriage and family.
If you are not whole, you have nothing to give to a spouse, your children, or to your new children. Instead, you wind up being a taker in the relationship.

This section will focus on identifying any areas in your life that need to be healed, whether from your childhood, failures in life or a previous broken relationship.

A. God made you to have fellowship with Him through a personal relationship with Jesus.
God has created us with a spirit (created in His likeness), and only a relationship with Him can fulfill your spirit.
When we try to fill our emptiness through relationships with men and women, we always come up empty and disappointed.

Through Jesus, you are a child of the living God. Jesus is always forgiving, always loving, always extending His grace to our lives. He looks at us and sees potential, not failure.

Commit yourself to spending more time in prayer and reading God's Word. Build a personal relationship with Jesus. It is through this process that we are made whole!!

B. Do not carry your past into your future and new family.
If you are remarried but still carry hurt, anger, bitterness, low self-esteem or resentment toward others from your past, those negative feelings will adversely affect everyone around you.

God needs time to heal your past hurts.
God wants to heal you from:

REJECTION	ANGER	JEALOUSY
RESENTMENT	CRITICISM	ENVY
REVENGE	GUILT	BITTERNESS

GET RID OF YOUR FAILURE MENTALITY!
YOU HAVE NOT MESSED UP TOO BAD IN GOD'S EYES.
GOD LOVES US AS HIS OWN, EVEN WHEN WE ARE NOT "LOVELY"!

NOW IS THE TIME TO BE SET FREE.

Jesus has a gracious way of restoring us when we fail or have experienced failure.
He does not criticize us.   He does not condemn us.
He does not humiliate us.   He does not harm us.
He does not even think bad thoughts about us.
He renews His mercy and grace to us each morning.
He gently takes us aside and asks us to reaffirm our love for Him.

Read John 18: 17, 25-27 and John 21: 15-18
Even after Peter had betrayed Jesus 3 times, Jesus reached out to Peter.

Read John 8: 3-11
An adulteress is brought to Jesus, yet He does not condemn her.

Answer the following questions:	**HUSBAND**	**WIFE**
1. Do you still have negative feelings toward your former spouse?	_____	_____
2. Do you take your anger out on your loved ones?	_____	_____
3. Do you feel like a failure?	_____	_____
4. Do you have low self-esteem?	_____	_____
5. Do you criticize others?	_____	_____
6. Do you want things done your way?	_____	_____
7. Do you often feel oppressed or depressed?	_____	_____
8. Do you avoid your parents or other family members?	_____	_____

Take the next few minutes in prayer asking God to forgive you, and to help you with any unforgiveness, anger, resentment, bitterness, jealousy, envy, etc.
Reaffirm your love and commitment to God.

II. God as the Center of the Family
GOD BREATHES ON BLENDED FAMILIES pages 49-50

Psalm 127: 1 states, *"Unless the LORD builds the house, they labor in vain who build it; unless the LORD guards the city, the watchman stays awake in vain."*

1 Corinthians 3: 11 says, *"For no one can lay any foundation other than the one already laid, which is Christ Jesus."*

Read pages 49–50 of the book.

If God is truly made the center of your home, your home will prosper.

Read Psalm 1: 1-3
Now read it again, replacing "man/ he/ his" with "family/ family's". Psalm 1: 1-3 (modified)

Your family needs to establish a standard of righteousness (right choices) and excellence.　> Spend time with God each day
　　　　　　> Be cautious of what your family watches on TV.
　　　　　　> Find a church that "challenges" your family to follow God's principles.
　　　　　　> Make a prayer time with family members.
　　　　　　> Be an example of Christ to your children.
　　　　　　> Hug your family; HUG = Hold Up Grace.
　　　　　　> Servanthood – As a family, serve in your church or community.

What are you doing now to establish a high moral standard in your home?

_____
_____
_____

What else can you do to make your home more God-centered?_____
_____
_____
_____
_____

III. An Orderly Home
GOD BREATHES ON BLENDED FAMILIES pages 50-51

Order is not just neatness.
Read through the list on page 51 of the BOOK.

Does your home have order as described on page 51? What changes do you need to make?_____
_____
_____

Discuss with your spouse any changes needed in your family to bring order, and write them down:_____

_____

_____

IV. Giving
GOD BREATHES ON BLENDED FAMILIES pages 52-53

The relationships that last are giving relationships.
Giving is a choice.
Giving is your key to receiving.
True giving expects nothing in return.
Giving "in" is a necessary part of giving.

"Until you are on your knees and have washed her feet, you have more to give, and you will only receive in accordance with your level of giving."

List ways that you are giving of yourself to your spouse and family members:
HUSBAND

_____

_____

_____

_____

_____

WIFE

_____

_____

_____

_____

_____

Think of new, creative ways to give of yourself to build a strong, loving family:
HUSBAND

_____

_____

_____

_____

WIFE

_____

_____

_____

_____

_____

V.   Silence
GOD BREATHES ON BLENDED FAMILIES pages 53-54

Read James 1: 19-20
SLOW TO SPEAK means SHUT UP!!!
When your negative emotions run high, do not react hastily.
The object of this scripture is not to stop communication --- the object is to avoid saying things that will hurt your loved ones, and cause damage to your relationship with your spouse or children.
Remember – damaged relationships are not quickly or easily restored.

VI.   High Grace
GOD BREATHES ON BLENDED FAMILIES pages 54-55

Write your own definition of "grace":
WIFE _____

_____

_____

HUSBAND _____

_____

_____

Think about a time in your life when God, or someone, extended grace to you. Write a brief description of that incident:
HUSBAND _____

_____

_____

WIFE _____

_____

_____

Discuss the parable of the unmerciful servant (Matthew 18: 23-30), and write down key thoughts:
WIFE _____

_____

_____

HUSBAND _____

_____

_____

Think about an incident when you missed an opportunity to extend grace to someone. Write it down:
HUSBAND _____

_____

_____

WIFE _____

_____

_____

We have been forgiven so generously and so many times, yet we get aggravated with or discipline our children over small, and sometimes insignificant things.

Grace is the result of love!   Love is the result of choice!
Grace is looking beyond faults!   Tolerance is biting your lip!

We are gracious to those who we love, and only tolerant to those who we do not love.

For grace to flow from you, you need to love those around you!

HOMEWORK:

1. Pray together with your spouse for at least 30 minutes!

2. Build your individual fellowship with God by committing 30 minutes more time each day than you do now.

3. Pray for those in your family who you do not love as you should, or who you sense a personality conflict with.

4. If you do not attend church, find one and take your whole family.

5. Develop new moral rules for your family.

6. Find a place to serve in your church or serve the needy in your community, and involve your children.

7. Read Chapter 5 of GOD BREATHES ON BLENDED FAMILIES for next week.

GOD BREATHES ON BLENDED FAMILIES WORKBOOK

Session 6

Opener   (See Appendix C -   Drama 2)

Act out or discuss this scene:
A stepfather is trying to develop a relationship with his new stepdaughter.
His stepdaughter is completely resistant to the relationship, and does not want him in her life. He is "in the way" and a "problem" in her life!
It ends with her being rude and walking out. He sits disappointed, and does not know what to try next.
1. What did you observe?_____
2. What emotions are each one feeling?_____
    Step-Daughter_____
    Step-Dad_____
3. What are some solutions?_____
    _____
    _____

  Her mother (natural parent) needs to: > set expectations.
  > explain the value that her husband brings.
  > demand respect from her daughter.

Review previous homework assignment.

Chapter 5   The Children's Perspective
GOD BREATHES ON BLENDED FAMILIES pages 56-66

Write the names of your natural and new children, and how you perceive each is adapting to your new family:
HUSBAND_____
_____
_____
_____
_____
WIFE_____
_____
_____
_____
_____
_____

What is your perspective on why each child <u>is, or is not</u> adapting?

WIFE _____

_____

_____

_____

_____

HUSBAND _____

_____

_____

_____

_____

If you have been through divorce, do you agree that your children were hurt from the divorce? <u>HUSBAND</u> _____ <u>WIFE</u> _____

> They were likely hurt more than you are aware of!

> Often children are shocked by the announcement of their parents' divorce.

> The "remarriage" and "new environment" has also affected your children.

> Children often do not tell their parents how they feel/ felt until years later.

> Behavioral signals – grades, disrespect, non-involvement with family.

> It is the parent's responsibility to help children heal from the divorce and prepare them for a new family.

Children of divorce have these things in common:

They do not have much to celebrate!

They must have hope!

They must have healing!

Everyone needs hope and healing in his or her life. Even King David, a man after God's own heart, needed hope and healing. In Psalm 37: 13, David declared*,*

"I am still confident of this: I will see the goodness of the Lord in the land of the living."

After his divorce from his former spouse, Moe had prayed*, "I am determined to see something good come from this divorce."*

God has a prosperous plan for your children. God wants to use you and your new family as an instrument of His hope and healing in their lives!

Early in our marriage, we gathered our young children and sat on our living room floor in a circle. We apologized to <u>each</u> child for the fact that he or she had been put through divorce. We let them share their heart. We all cried. We prayed for each one.

To better understand the children in your new family and what they may be feeling, read the next sections in GOD BREATHES ON BLENDED FAMILIES, beginning on page 58.

Discuss each topic with your spouse or group, and make personal observations of your family. Write them down:

Need for a Strong Family Environment (Page 58)

_____
_____
_____

If the only love the child feels in the new home is from his or her natural parent, the home atmosphere is divided.

Dealing with Varied Disciplines (Page 59)

_____
_____
_____

Someone is Always Missing (Page 60-61)

_____
_____
_____

"After all those back-and-forth flights, I've learned NOT to get too emotionally attached." Children of divorce lead complicated lives, logistically and emotionally.

The Other Natural Parent (Page 61-62)

_____
_____
_____

Your former spouse may have caused great pain in your life. But if you are not walking in forgiveness, you are only hurting yourself and your children. Holding a grudge will choke the life out of you, your natural children, and your new family.

Special Events (Page 63-64)

_____
_____
_____

The Pawn (Page 65-66)

_____
_____
_____

Questions about your children:
Do you know how your natural child/ children were feeling when you remarried?
DAD_____

_____

MOM_____

_____
_____

Have you helped your natural children heal from the divorce?

MOM

_____

DAD

_____

Did you prepare your children for the new marriage and family environment? (Possible new home location, change in schools, leaving old friends, making new friends, etc.)

DAD

_____

MOM

_____

What have you, as a parent/ stepparent, done to help your children feel a part of your new family?

WIFE

_____

_____

HUSBAND

_____

_____

Have you, as a parent/ stepparent, done anything to make your new children not want to connect to you or your new home?

WIFE

_____

_____

HUSBAND

_____

_____

Have your children done anything to disrespect your new spouse or new children?

DAD

_____

_____

MOM

_____

_____

Have you used your natural children as a communication tool, so you did not have to speak with your former spouse?

MOM

_____

DAD

_____

HOMEWORK:

1. Pray each day with your spouse --- and for each child.

2. Complete your answers to all of the questions about your children (above), and discuss actions you can take to help your children heal and feel a vital part of your new family.

3. Have a family meeting and apologize for the hurts in your children's lives. Express your desire to your children to want to become a real family.

4. Read Chapter 6 of GOD BREATHES ON BLENDED FAMILIES for next week.

GOD BREATHES ON BLENDED FAMILIES WORKBOOK

Session 7

Opener

Case Study: A couple named Pete and Rita married. Pete had three children from his previous marriage. Rita had a four-year-old son with a man she never married. The boy's natural father had no contact with him.

Pete decided to adopt Rita's son. They hired an attorney to begin adoption proceedings, and performed all the legal obligations to find the father of the boy to get his permission. The father was never found, and the day of adoption came.

The judge explained to Pete the rights of adoption as follows:

1. The legal adoption could never be cancelled or nullified.
2. Pete could never emancipate his adopted son, as he could his own children.
3. Pete could never leave his adopted son out of his inheritance, as he could his own children.

Please share your thoughts about this case.

Review previous homework assignment.

Chapter 6   Responsibilities of a Stepparent
GOD BREATHES ON BLENDED FAMILIES pages 67-80

Loving and parenting a child who was not born to you is not a natural thing.
> It is often "out-of-the-norm" and "out-of-our-comfort-zone".

Children are very important to God.

Read Luke 18: 15-16.   {this passage is recorded in 3 of the 4 Gospels}

Do not hinder the little children --- it is not easy because they can be disturbing, distracting and demanding.
Jesus' disciples did not understand Jesus' mission, objective and strategy. As parents and stepparents, we often do not understand the importance of our children, and the impact of our roles in their lives.

Read Psalm 127: 3

Stepchildren are also a reward from the Lord.
They are NOT extra baggage, someone else's problem, or along for the ride.

God has given you a second chance in your remarriage, and new children with it.

Regardless of intention, stepparents will have a positive or negative impact on their stepchildren.

We are to serve our children, to love them, to bless them, to nurture them, and to help them in every way possible. We are to lead them along the right paths in life.

The goal of this chapter is not to teach you how to be a good stepparent.
Rather, the goal is to move you from being a stepparent to being a parent to all children in your home or care.

Overcoming the "stepparent syndrome" takes effort, time and God's favor on your life. All three are equally important.

We, as Christians, can accomplish much because we are children of God, and He grants us favor with God and with men.
Read Luke 2: 52_____
If we ask Him, He will give us favor with our new children.
As Christians, we are overcomers!

What kind of resistance or frustration have you encountered thus far in your role as a new parent?
HUSBAND

_____
_____
_____
_____

WIFE

_____
_____
_____
_____

I.   A "Spirit" of Adoption
GOD BREATHES ON BLENDED FAMILIES pages 68-71

In the opener, we discussed a case study about legal adoption.

Define "adoption" in your own words:_____
_____
_____

36

Adopt --- Latin "adoptare" = TO CHOOSE
        --- Webster = TO TAKE BY CHOICE INTO A RELATIONSHIP

Read and discuss Galatians 4: 6, 2 Corinthians 6: 18, and 1Peter 2: 9   (BOOK page 69)
        God chose you as His very own.
        You belong to God.
        God has called you into His light.

God expects us to do for others what He has already done for us.
We need to mentally and emotionally adopt (choose) our new children.

Those precious little ones (even the older ones) who are now living with you as part of your family, are waiting for you to call them into your light - your world - your love.   Make a choice to choose them.

Has the spirit of adoption infected your new family yet? **HUSBAND**   **WIFE**

If you do not have this spirit of adoption toward your new children, ask God to help you find it. Just the conscious act of asking for God's help in prayer will unify your family in an incredible way!

Review Advice on page 70.

        Do not expect anything in return. This is your seedtime >> your harvest will come!
        Anniversaries – include your new children ("Anniversary of your life with them!")

II.   *Jesus Had a Stepparent*

Write down your response/ reaction to this next statement:
"Jesus was a stepchild to Joseph and part of a blended family."_____
_____
_____

Had you previously thought about the fact that Jesus was raised by Joseph, his stepfather?_____

Story of Joseph and his relationship to Jesus:
Read Matthew 1: 16-24 and Luke 1: 26-27
Read Luke Chapter 2 - (Not in Appendix A)
A. Joseph's initial reaction
        Not my child.   Planned to send Mary away.   Confusion.

B. Angel visited and instructed Joseph
        Child was from God.   Marry Mary.   <u>You</u> are to name Him Jesus.

C. Joseph's Legacy
Given responsibility to name Jesus --- a role of "fathers" in Israelite custom.

Luke 3: 23b says, *"He(Jesus) was the son, so it was thought, of Joseph."*
In Matthew 1: 16, Joseph is listed in the lineage of Jesus.
Joseph's recorded legacy is based on his role and responsibility toward his stepson, not his natural children.

You may think, "But Jesus was GOD's Son." → So are your stepchildren!

III.   Responsibilities of a New Father
GOD BREATHES ON BLENDED FAMILIES pages 71-76

Dad, if you have a natural son or daughter, list the responsibilities you have as a father:
DAD _____
_____
_____
_____

Now, list the responsibilities you have as a new parent to your new children:
DAD _____
_____
_____
_____

Dad, your responsibilities should be the same in both cases!

Fathers provide three things to their children:
1. Provision – spiritually and financially
2. Identity – belonging, importance and significance {Becnel/ Morriz family – no longer just the Becnel home}
3. Security – safe, peaceful and loving environment; PRODUCES COURAGE

Just as Joseph was responsible for Jesus, you are responsible for the well being of each member of your new family. You are not taking the place of your new children's birth father, but you have just as much influence over them.

Some children have a hard time accepting a new father figure. Understand that they did not choose you; you chose their mother and she chose you.

IV.   The Role of a Stepmother
GOD BREATHES ON BLENDED FAMILIES pages 76-80

When you hear the word, "stepmother" what is your first thought?_____

Her efforts are often sabotaged. *No matter how hard she tries, nothing she does is ever good enough, especially when her efforts are compared to those of the children's natural mother.*

She is often told, "It is not your responsibility."

Eventually, Paige realized that, *"I was not replacing their mother, but that I had been given the chance to nurture and help raise a part of Moe."*
A wife and mother is the very backbone of the home!

Mothers provide three things to their children:
1. A "nesting" instinct that turns a house into a home.
2. Intuition – a sense about things that serves as a warning for the family.
3. Spiritual sensitivity – women tend to be more spiritually connected than men.

Mom, if you have a natural son or daughter, list the responsibilities you have as a mother:
MOM _____

_____

_____

Now, list the responsibilities you have as a new parent to your new children:
MOM _____

_____

_____

Your responsibilities should be the same in both cases!

V.   *Accepting Your Assignment:*

Stepparents, are you willing to accept your assignments?
HUSBAND _____   **WIFE** _____

Discuss these questions with your spouse:
1. If your spouse has children, does your spouse need and/or hope that you will accept the awesome role of being a loving, caring parent to their children in your new home?
   WIFE _____   **HUSBAND** _____

2. If YES, does this mean that your role as new parent to your spouse's children is to take over the role of the children's other parent?
   HUSBAND _____   **WIFE** _____

3. Compare the role you have with your new children, to the role that God gave to Joseph.

HUSBAND _____

_____

WIFE _____

_____

_____

As parents, we are here to serve our children, to bless them, to love them, to nurture them, and to help them in every way possible!

HOMEWORK:

1. Pray with your spouse for your roles as new parents.

2. Make the choice to mentally and spiritually adopt your new children.

3. Take your new children on a "friendship" date. Spend one-on-one time with each of them to build relationship with them.

4. Read Chapter 7 of GOD BREATHES ON BLENDED FAMILIES for next week.

GOD BREATHES ON BLENDED FAMILIES WORKBOOK

Session 8

Opener

Act out or discuss this situation:
Barry takes Kate (his new wife), children and stepchildren to his Dad's family reunion. As Barry mingles with his family members, Barry's mother (Kate's mother-in-law) separately confronts Kate. She tells Kate that Barry does not visit her as much as when he was a single parent, and she blames Kate for the change in Barry's behavior.
Kate begins to feel very uncomfortable and tells Barry what just happened. Kate is very upset and is ready to leave, but Barry is not because it is his Dad's family reunion, and he wants to visit with aunts, uncles and cousins he has not seen in 6 years.

How is Kate feeling?_____
How is Barry feeling?_____
Give your suggestions on resolving this situation.

_____

_____

Review previous homework assignment.

Chapter 7   Interference from Extended Family
GOD BREATHES ON BLENDED FAMILIES pages 81-88

We pray that your family does not need the advice found in this chapter. However, all families need to be on guard to protect their families from all hurtful influences.

Let's proceed with caution! You do not want to create any strife with your extended family. It may take some time for your extended family to love and accept your new spouse and children --- so:
> *Give your extended family the benefit of the doubt.*
> *Give your extended family time to develop a relationship with your new spouse and children!*

I. Non-acceptance of your new spouse and children

Look for the symptoms of harmful behavior from your extended family members:

Do your parents accept your new spouse as a family member?
HUSBAND_____
WIFE_____

41

Do your siblings accept your new spouse as family?

WIFE _____

HUSBAND _____

How do your brothers and sisters respond to your new children?

HUSBAND _____

WIFE _____

How do your parents treat your new children? Do they treat your new children the same as your natural children?

HUSBAND _____

WIFE _____

Are your spouse and all children treated equally by family during the holidays?

WIFE _____

HUSBAND _____

If your answers to any of these questions were negative, we suggest that you meet with your family and let them know how you feel. Explain to them how important they are to your new family, and how you need them to help you make your new marriage and family work.

If talking to your family does not produce any improvement, continue to love and pray for your extended family.

II.   *Honoring vs. Obeying - Avoiding Controlling Parents*
GOD BREATHES ON BLENDED FAMILIES pages 85-86

Review the definitions of "honor" and "obey" on page 85 of the BOOK.

Do you feel your parents control your life? If yes, how?

WIFE _____

_____

_____

HUSBAND _____

_____

_____

Does your spouse feel your parents are trying to control you or your marriage?   If yes, how?

YOUR HUSBAND _____

_____

_____

YOUR WIFE _____

_____

_____

If you answered YES to either of these questions, have you met with your parents to discuss your feelings, and the negative impact their actions have on your new family?

HUSBAND

_____

WIFE

_____

III.   Standing Up for Your New Family

If your extended family is causing hurt to your new spouse and children, it is your responsibility to protect your new spouse and children from their harmful acts. You have the responsibility to guard your new family against hurt from all outside influences. If you do not guard your family, you then become another instrument of hurt to them.

Are you aware of any rejection or hurt feelings being created in your new family by your extended family or friends? If so, what and by whom?

WIFE

_____

HUSBAND

_____

Identify any extended family members who have not accepted your new spouse or new children.

HUSBAND

_____

WIFE

_____

Your ultimate goal is that your extended family would love, embrace and be a part of your new family, and that your new family would love, embrace and accept them also!!!
    Remember, God wants to bring healing and complete restoration. Walk in love toward everyone, even those trying to bring division in your life.

What have you done, or can you do to reach out to difficult extended family members?

Taking them to dinner?	_____
Sending them flowers?	_____
Baby-sitting their children one night?	_____
Being there for them in a time of need?	_____
Offering to pray for any special needs?	_____
Other?	_____

HOMEWORK:

1. Pray for unity with your extended family, and acceptance by your extended family!
2. Reach out to a difficult family member using one of the above ideas, or your own.
3. Read Chapters 8 and 9 of GOD BREATHES ON BLENDED FAMILIES for next week.

GOD BREATHES ON BLENDED FAMILIES WORKBOOK

Session 9

Opener

1. Have each stepparent say something positive about each of his or her stepchildren (new children)!

Attributes_____   Talents_____
Their heart_____   Abilities_____
Something good they did_____   A Good Habit_____

2. Also, have each stepparent share a good moment they have had with each new child!

_____
_____
_____
_____

Review previous homework assignment.

Chapter 8   Vision and Purpose
GOD BREATHES ON BLENDED FAMILIES pages 89-94

I.   *Planning for Your Family Success*

People never plan to fail; they simply fail to plan. This also applies to families and relationships. Consider New Year's resolutions that are seldom achieved.

The reason people and relationships fail is because they have no vision (or no common vision), and therefore no goals (or different goals).

People need a purpose for their lives other than simply satisfying their own wants. Without purpose, we lead a very unfulfilled life. And if we are unfulfilled, our marriage and family will be unfulfilled.

Churches that have cell groups know that the groups will eventually dissolve if they have no outlet to serve the community or needy people. In our former church, every cell group was given a goal to serve in some capacity at least once a month.

Children need to see their parents serving others. It is through our giving that we receive.

44

Go back to the vision and purpose you wrote for your family in Session 4 - Chapter 3, and copy it in the space below:

_____

_____

_____

_____

_____

Based on what you have learned in the last 8 weeks, does it need to be modified? If so, do it now.

II. *Write a Family Mission Statement*

In order to help establish common vision and goals, we suggest you try writing a Mission Statement for your family.

A Mission Statement is a written declaration, usually one or two sentences, describing the goals and objectives of an entity. Its purpose is to bring focus to accomplishing goals, needs and desired characteristics in your family.

Read the Becnel Family Mission Statement on page 91 of the BOOK.

Every family could have multiple Mission Statements --- discussing such areas as spiritual, family planning, educational, financial, employment, and retirement goals.

Include the entire family in developing the statement! Allow your children to contribute to the Mission Statement. This process will open communication between you, your spouse, and your children. It will also bring agreement and focus to your family.

Developing your family Mission Statement will reveal divisions, conflicting goals and solutions to existing problems.

Read page 93 of the BOOK for some key components that your family should pursue. Include these in your Mission Statement.

With your spouse, begin a draft of a Mission Statement.

_____

_____

_____

_____

_____

_____

_____

_____

_____

III.   *Strategy*
GOD BREATHES ON BLENDED FAMILIES page 92

How will you achieve your family Mission? Identify actions and changes that your family needs to take to achieve the Mission. Write down your strategy:

_____
_____
_____
_____
_____
_____
_____

HOMEWORK:

1. Have a family meeting to complete your Mission Statement. Let each family member give input, and add at least part of each child's input to the Statement. This will cause them to feel a real part of your family, and to take ownership of the family goals.

2. Pray with your family that God's purpose for your family would be revealed.

Chapter 9   Prayer --- An Awesome Thing
GOD BREATHES ON BLENDED FAMILIES pages 95-100

I.   *Making Prayer an Integral Part of Your Life*

There were many days when we (the Becnel's) had no more emotional strength to continue trying to build our family. The struggles were frequent and intense!

Read Ephesians 6: 12.
Your fight is not against each other, but against Satan and his army, who look for every opportunity to divide your marriage and family.

II.   *The Circle of Influence*

On the opposite page draw a large circle. Now draw a smaller circle inside the large circle. Draw you and your family in the center.
Within the inner circle, write those things in life that you have direct control of.
Between the inner and outer circle, write those things in life that you do not have direct control of.
Prayer over both areas will change your life!!!
God operates when we give Him control, or when we have no control. If you are determined to try to fix it yourself, He will let you.

III. Prayer Initiates Positive Change

Insanity has been described as "doing the same thing over and over and expecting different results." The same is true of our prayer life.

If we pray the same amount of time, with the same lack of zeal, with the same weak sacrifice and the same level of distraction, we cannot and will not experience change.

If you need radical change in your life, your marriage, your new family, or your children, you need to radically change your approach to prayer.

Prayer has been the overwhelming power that has produced the positive change in our hearts first, and then in our blended family.

You can initiate positive change in yourself and your family.

Making prayer a larger part of your life will require change. People resist change!

Read Luke 11: 2-4   How to pray

Read Luke 11: 5-13   Benefit of prayer

IV. Hold Your Family Up in Prayer

In the lines below, list needs and desires for each area identified:

For Yourself

_____

_____

For Your Spouse

_____

_____

For Your Spouse's Dreams/ Goals

_____

_____

For Your Family to Become All God Wants it To Be

_____

_____

For Your Family Issues

_____

_____

For Your Role in the New Home

_____

_____

For a Spirit of Adoption

_____

_____

For Your Children's Needs

_____

_____

For a Spirit of Acceptance and High Respect for Each Other

_____

_____

For The Spirit of Christ in Each Family Member (Galatians 5: 22-23)

_____

_____

For Your Family Purpose and Goals

_____

_____

For a Spirit of Inward Servanthood

_____

_____

For an Outward Avenue to Serve Others as a Family

_____

_____

V.   Silence – And Listen

a) Do not close your prayer time when you are finished talking to God.
   Stop – and wait on God for your instruction, solutions and direction. God's Holy Spirit
   will speak the answers to your family issues into your thoughts.
b) Get pen and paper, and write down the answers and ideas as they come to you.

VI.   Teaching Your Children How to Pray

a) Wake them up and let them join you and your spouse in morning prayer. (Do not
    expect your young children to pray more than 10-15 minutes, depending on age.
    Consider their limited "attention span.")
b) Take them to morning prayer at your church.
c) Take them to prayer meetings.
d) Start a family devotional time at home.

VII. P.U.S.H.

Pray   **U**ntil   **S**omething   **H**appens

Push through every situation in prayer!
When you have had a good day, PRAY.
When you have had a bad day, PRAY.
When you have had another fight, PRAY.
When you cannot go another day, PRAY.

Eventually you will see the giant walls crumble into a pile of dust!
Gradually, yet certainly, your family will sense a dramatic, positive change.
Soon, God's Breath will begin turning all hard hearts into vessels of honor.

VIII. Resolving Conflicts in Life (See Appendix B)

Read and discuss the article in Appendix B.

DO NOT GIVE UP!

NEVER GIVE UP, NO MATTER WHAT!

Almighty God is Working on Your Behalf!

Allow God to Separate and Change Your Heart!

God's BREATH Will Create Abundant Life in Your Family!

THERE IS NOTHING TOO DIFFICULT FOR HIM!

Appendix A
Scripture References

Session 1

Psalm 28: 7 The LORD is my strength and my shield; my heart trusted in Him, and I am helped; therefore my heart greatly rejoices, and with my song I will praise Him.

Psalm 34: 18 The LORD is near to those who have a broken heart, and saves such as have a contrite spirit.

Isaiah 42: 16 I will bring the blind by a way they did not know; I will lead them in paths they have not known. I will make darkness light before them, and crooked places straight. These things I will do for them, and not forsake them.

John 14: 26 But the Helper, the Holy Spirit, whom the Father will send in My name, He will teach you all things, and bring to your remembrance all things that I said to you.

Romans 8: 34 Who is he who condemns? It is Christ who died, and furthermore is also risen, who is even at the right hand of God, who also makes intercession for us.

Mark 10: 6-9 But from the beginning of the creation, God made them male and female. For this reason a man shall leave his father and mother and be joined to his wife, and the two shall become one flesh; so then they are no longer two, but one flesh. Therefore what God has joined together, let not man separate.

Ecclesiastes 4: 9-10 Two are better than one, because they have a good reward for their labor. For if they fall, one will lift up his companion. But woe to him who is alone when he falls, for he has no one to help him up.

2 Chronicles 20: 12-15 O our God, will You not judge them? For we have no power against this great multitude that is coming against us; nor do we know what to do, but our eyes are upon You. Now all Judah, with their little ones, their wives, and their children, stood before the LORD. Then the Spirit of the LORD came upon Jahaziel the son of Zechariah, the son of Benaiah, the son of Jeiel, the son of Mattaniah, a Levite of the sons of Asaph, in the midst of the assembly. And he said, "Listen, all you of Judah and you inhabitants of Jerusalem, and you, King Jehoshaphat! Thus says the LORD to you: "Do not be afraid nor dismayed because of this great multitude, for the battle is not yours, but God's."

1 Chronicles 5: 20 And they were helped against them, and the Hagrites were delivered into their hand, and all who were with them, for they cried out to God in the battle. He heeded their prayer, because they put their trust in Him.

Philippians 4: 6-7 Be anxious for nothing, but in everything by prayer and supplication, with thanksgiving, let your requests be made known to God; and the peace of God, which surpasses all understanding, will guard your hearts and minds through Christ Jesus.

1 John 1: 9 If we confess our sins, He is faithful and just to forgive us our sins and to cleanse us from all unrighteousness.

Psalm 103: 12 As far as the east is from the west, so far has He removed our transgressions from us.

Psalm 103: 4-8 Who redeems your life from destruction, who crowns you with loving-kindness and tender mercies, who satisfies your mouth with good things, so that your youth is renewed like the eagle's. The LORD executes righteousness and justice for all who are oppressed. He made known His ways to Moses, His acts to the children of Israel. The LORD is merciful and gracious, slow to anger, and abounding in mercy.

John 10: 10 The thief does not come except to steal, and to kill, and to destroy. I have come that they may have life, and that they may have it more abundantly.

1 Corinthians 13: 4-6 Love suffers long and is kind; love does not envy; love does not parade itself, is not puffed up; does not behave rudely, does not seek its own, is not provoked, thinks no evil; does not rejoice in iniquity, but rejoices in the truth;

Session 2

Proverbs 13: 10 Pride only breeds quarrels, but wisdom is found in those who take advice.

Genesis 21: 8-14 The child (Isaac) grew and was weaned, and on the day Isaac was weaned, Abraham held a great feast. But Sarah saw that the son whom Hagar the Egyptian had borne to Abraham was mocking, and she said the Abraham, "Get rid of that slave woman and her son, for that slave woman's son will never share in the inheritance with my son Isaac."
The matter distressed Abraham greatly because it concerned his son. But God said to him, "Do not be so distressed about the boy and your maidservant. Listen to whatever Sarah tells you, because it is through Isaac that your offspring will be reckoned. I will make the son of the maidservant into a nation also, because he is your offspring."
Early the next morning Abraham took some food and a skin of water and gave them to Hagar. He set them on her shoulders and then sent her off with the boy. She went on her way and wandered in the desert of Beersheba.

Jeremiah 1: 5 Before I formed you in the womb I knew you; before you were born I sanctified you; I ordained you a prophet to the nations."

Jeremiah 29: 11 For I know the thoughts that I think toward you, says the LORD, thoughts of peace and not of evil, to give you a future and a hope.

Isaiah 55: 9 "As the heavens are higher than the earth, so are my ways higher than your ways and my thoughts than your thoughts."

Session 3

Genesis 2: 22-24 Then the rib which the LORD God had taken from man He made into a woman, and He brought her to the man. And Adam said: "This is now bone of my bones and flesh of my flesh; she shall be called Woman, because she was taken out of Man." Therefore a man shall leave his father and mother and be joined to his wife, and they shall become one flesh.

Philippians 2: 1-2 If you have any encouragement from being united with Christ, if any comfort from his love, if any fellowship with the Spirit, if any tenderness and compassion, then make my joy complete by being like-minded, having the same love, being one in spirit and purpose.

John 3:16 For God so loved the world that He gave His only begotten Son, that whoever believes in Him should not perish but have everlasting life

Galatians 3: 26 For you are all sons of God through faith in Christ Jesus.

Matthew 28: 18-20 And Jesus came and spoke to them, saying, "All authority has been given to Me in heaven and on earth. Therefore go and make disciples of all nations, baptizing them in the name of the Father and of the Son and of the Holy Spirit, and teaching them to obey everything I have commanded you. And surely I am with you always, to the very end of the age."

Genesis 1: 27 So God created man in His own image; in the image of God He created him; male and female He created them.

Romans 8: 29 For whom He foreknew, He also predestined to be conformed to the image of His Son, that He might be the firstborn among many brethren.

Jeremiah 29: 11 For I know the thoughts that I think toward you, says the LORD, thoughts of peace and not of evil, to give you a future and a hope.

Mark 16: 15-18 And He said to them, "Go into all the world and preach the gospel to every creature. He who believes and is baptized will be saved; but he who does not believe will be condemned. And these signs will follow those who believe: In My name they will cast out demons; they will speak with new tongues; they will take up serpents; and if they drink anything deadly, it will by no means hurt them; they will lay hands on the sick, and they will recover."

Deuteronomy 14: 2 For you are a holy people to the LORD your God, and the LORD has chosen you to be a people for Himself, a special treasure above all the peoples who are on the face of the earth.

2 Corinthians 6: 18 "I will be a Father to you, and you shall be My sons and daughters, says the LORD Almighty."

John 15: 15 No longer do I call you servants, for a servant does not know what his master is doing; but I have called you friends, for all things that I heard from My Father I have made known to you.

Ephesians 5: 25 Husbands, love your wives, just as Christ also loved the church and gave Himself for her.

Ephesians 6:12 For our struggle is not against flesh and blood, but against the rulers, against the authorities, against the powers of this dark world and against the spiritual forces of evil in the heavenly realms.

Session 4

1 Peter 5: 8 Be sober, be vigilant; because your adversary the devil walks about like a roaring lion, seeking whom he may devour.

Ephesians 6: 12 For we do not wrestle against flesh and blood, but against principalities, against powers, against the rulers of the darkness of this age, against spiritual hosts of wickedness in the heavenly places.

Psalm 127: 1 "Unless the Lord builds the house, its builders labor in vain."

Matthew 12: 25 Jesus knew their thoughts and said to them, "every kingdom divided against itself will be ruined, and every city or household divided against itself will not stand."

Psalm 37: 4- 5 Delight yourself also in the LORD, and He shall give you the desires of your heart. Commit your way to the LORD, Trust also in Him, and He shall bring it to pass.

Session 5

John 18: 17, 25-27 (Peter Denies Jesus Three Times)
17) Then the servant girl who kept the door said to Peter, "You are not also one of this Man's disciples, are you?" He said, "I am not."
25-27) Now Simon Peter stood and warmed himself. Therefore they said to him, "You are not also one of His disciples, are you?" He denied it and said, "I am not!"
One of the servants of the high priest, a relative of him whose ear Peter cut off, said, "Did I not see you in the garden with Him?" Peter then denied again; and immediately a rooster crowed.

John 21: 15-18 So when they had eaten breakfast, Jesus said to Simon Peter, "Simon, son of Jonah, do you love Me more than these?" He said to Him, "Yes, Lord; You know that I love You." He said to him, "Feed My lambs." He said to him again a second time, "Simon, son of Jonah, do you love Me?" He said to Him, "Yes, Lord; You know that I love You." He said to him, "Tend My sheep." He said to him the third time, "Simon, son of Jonah, do you love Me?" Peter was grieved because He said to him the third time, "Do you love Me?" And he said to Him, "Lord, You know all things; You know that I love You."
Jesus said to him, "Feed My sheep. Most assuredly, I say to you, when you were younger, you girded yourself and walked where you wished; but when you are old, you will stretch out your hands, and another will gird you and carry you where you do not wish.

John 8: 3-11 Then the scribes and Pharisees brought to Him a woman caught in adultery. And when they had set her in the midst, they said to Him, "Teacher, this woman was caught in adultery, in the very act. Now Moses, in the law, commanded us that such should be stoned. But what do You say?" This they said, testing Him, that they might have something of which to accuse Him. But Jesus stooped down and wrote on the ground with His finger, as though He did not hear. So when they continued asking Him, He raised Himself up and said to them, "He who is without sin among you, let him throw a stone at her first." And again He stooped down and wrote on the ground. Then those who heard it, being convicted by their conscience, went out one by one, beginning with the oldest even to the last. And Jesus was left alone, and the woman standing in the midst. When Jesus had raised Himself up and saw no one but the woman, He said to her, "Woman, where are those accusers of yours? Has no one condemned you?" She said, "No one, Lord." And Jesus said to her, "Neither do I condemn you; go and sin no more."

Psalm 1: 1-3 Blessed is the man who does not walk in the counsel of the wicked or stand in the way of sinners or sit in the seat of mockers. But his delight is in the law of the LORD, and on his law he meditates day and night. He is like a tree planted by streams of water, which yields its fruit in season and whose leaf does not wither. Whatever he does prospers.

Psalm 1: 1-3 (modified) Blessed is the *family* who does not walk in the counsel of the wicked or stand in the way of sinners or sit in the seat of mockers. But *that family's* delight is in the law of the LORD, and on his law *that family* meditates day and night. *That family* is like a tree planted by streams of water, which yields its fruit in season and whose leaf does not wither. Whatever *that family* does prospers.

James 1: 19-20 My dear brothers, take note of this: everyone should be quick to listen, slow to speak and slow to get angry, for man's anger does not bring about the righteous life that God desires.

Matthew 18: 23-30 Therefore the kingdom of heaven is like a certain king who wanted to settle accounts with his servants. And when he had begun to settle accounts, one was brought to him who owed him ten thousand talents. But as he was not able to pay, his master commanded that he be sold, with his wife and children and all that he had, and that payment be made. The servant therefore fell down before him, saying, "Master, have patience with me, and I will pay you all.' Then the master of that servant was moved with compassion, released him, and forgave him the debt. "But that servant went out and found one of his fellow servants who owed him a hundred denarii; and he laid hands on him and took him by the throat, saying, "Pay me what you owe!' So his fellow servant fell down at his feet and begged him, saying, "Have patience with me, and I will pay you all.' And he would not, but went and threw him into prison till he should pay the debt.

Session 6 – none

Session 7

Luke 18: 15-16 People were also bringing babies to Jesus to have Him touch them. When the disciples saw this, they rebuked them. But Jesus called the children to Him and said, "Let the little children come to Me, and do not hinder them, for the kingdom of God belongs to such as these".

Psalm 127: 3 Sons are a heritage from the Lord, children a reward from Him.

Galatians 4: 6 Because you are sons, God sent the Spirit of his Son into our hearts, the Spirit who calls out, "Abba, Father."

2 Corinthians 6: 18 "I will be a Father to you, and you will be my sons and daughters, says the Lord Almighty."

1 Peter 2: 9 But you are a chosen people, a royal priesthood, a holy nation, a people belonging to God, that you may declare the praises of him who called you out of darkness into his wonderful light.

Matthew 1: 16-24 and Jacob the father of Joseph, the husband of Mary, of whom was born Jesus, who is called Christ. Thus there were fourteen generations in all from Abraham to David, fourteen from David to the exile to Babylon, and fourteen from the exile to the Christ.
This is how the birth of Jesus Christ came about: His mother Mary was pledged to be married to Joseph, but before they came together, she was found to be with child through the Holy Spirit. Because Joseph her husband was a righteous man and did not want to expose her to public

disgrace, he had in mind to divorce her quietly. But after he had considered this, an angel of the Lord appeared to him in a dream and said, "Joseph son of David, do not be afraid to take Mary home as your wife, because what is conceived in her is from the Holy Spirit. 21She will give birth to a son, and you are to give him the name Jesus, because he will save his people from their sins." All this took place to fulfill what the Lord had said through the prophet: "The virgin will be with child and will give birth to a son, and they will call him Immanuel" --which means, "God with us." When Joseph woke up, he did what the angel of the Lord had commanded him and took Mary home as his wife.

Luke 1: 26-27 In the sixth month, God sent the angel Gabriel to Nazareth, a town in Galilee, to a virgin pledged to be married to a man named Joseph, a descendant of David. The virgin's name was Mary.

Luke 3:23 Now Jesus himself was about thirty years old when he began his ministry. He was the son, so it was thought, of Joseph,

Matthew 1: 16 and Jacob the father of Joseph, the husband of Mary, of whom was born Jesus, who is called Christ.

Session 8 - none

Session 9

Ephesians 6: 12 For we wrestle not against flesh and blood, but against the rulers, against the authorities, against the powers of this dark world and against the spiritual forces of evil in the heavenly realms.

Luke 11: 2-4 He (Jesus) said to them, "When you pray, say: 'Father, hallowed be your name, your kingdom come. Give us each day our daily bread. Forgive us our sins, for we also forgive everyone who sins against us. And lead us not into temptation.' "

Luke 11: 5-13 Then He (Jesus) said to them, "Suppose one of you has a friend, and he goes to him at midnight and says, 'Friend, lend me three loaves of bread, because a friend of mine on a journey has come to me, and I have nothing to set before him.'
"Then the one inside answers, 'Don't bother me. The door is already locked, and my children are with me in bed. I can't get up and give you anything.' I tell you, though he will not get up and give him the bread because he is his friend, yet because of the man's boldness he will get up and give him as much as he needs.
"So I say to you: Ask and it will be given to you; seek and you will find; knock and the door will be opened to you. 10For everyone who asks receives; he who seeks finds; and to him who knocks, the door will be opened.
"Which of you fathers, if your son asks for a fish, will give him a snake instead? Or if he asks for an egg, will give him a scorpion? If you then, though you are evil, know how to give good gifts to your children, how much more will your Father in heaven give the Holy Spirit to those who ask him!"

Galatians 5: 22-23 But the fruit of the Spirit is love, joy, peace, longsuffering, kindness, goodness, faithfulness, gentleness, self-control.

Appendix B
Article: Resolving Conflicts in Life
By Moe & Paige Becnel

We were recently asked, "How do you resolve conflicts?" Our immediate response was "That's a good question --- and we'll have to get back to you on that!"

Everyone experiences conflicts at different times in their life. You may have had conflicts at your job, with creditors, with businesses, and even with people at church.
Yet, the most devastating conflicts are found in families. Conflicts directly oppose the real purpose of a family. As long as a conflict is not properly resolved, the family and all family members suffer.

In researching the answer to the question, we found these Webster definitions ---
  Conflict: > a fighting or struggle for mastery;   > a combat
                  > a striving to oppose or overcome

  Resolve: > to do away with doubts or disputes;   > to clear of difficulties

  Resolution: > *a fixed purpose or determination of mind*
                  > the act of unraveling a perplexing question or problem.

Thus, conflicts involve a struggle created by opposing views, opinions or purposes. Your conflicts are driven by what you want, what others want that you are not willing to give, what you can get, and wanting things your way.

Business Conflict:
An example of a business conflict is when we go buy a car. The buyer's purpose is to get the best value for his money. The seller's purpose is to sell the car to the buyer at a price as close to the suggested retail price as possible. As such, buyer and seller often have conflicting goals!
Another example is conflict between employer and employee. There are management books that teach supervisors how to deal with employee conflicts. However, most teach conflict resolution as a learned process or formula that include negotiation skills, skills involving manipulation or even threats of disciplinary action. A Union contract negotiation is another example. The objective is to get at least part of what each side wants.

Enough about businesses --- in this article, we want to focus on key Biblical ingredients needed to successfully resolve conflict within ourselves and in families.

Personal Conflict:
Everyday, we face a struggle between what our flesh wants vs. what God's Spirit desires for our lives. The struggle between flesh and Spirit is described in the Holy Bible as the lust of the flesh, the lust of the eye and the pride of life.

Relationship Conflict:

James 4: 1-3 says, *"What causes fights and quarrels among you? Don't they come from your desires that battle within you? You want something but don't get it. You kill and covet, but you cannot have what you want. You quarrel and fight. You do not have because you do not ask. When you ask, you do not receive, because you ask with wrong motives, that you may spend what you get on your pleasures."*

One of the toughest situations is when two people you love are in conflict with each other, and you are in the middle. Children of divorce know all about this situation, as divorced parents are often in conflict with each other. Extended family can create similar situations.

According to the definition, resolution requires being of one mind and purpose with the other person. *We believe that true conflict resolution is not an art. It is also not a learned skill. Rather, it is an attitude of the heart!*

Key ingredients to successful conflict resolution:

1. *Relationships are of utmost value!*

   God is all about life-long relationships. All 10 Commandments to Israel from God dealt with relationships. The 1st four discuss our relationship with God. The other 6 discuss our relationships with people. All other issues are secondary to God.

   As Christians, we are to pursue the heart of God and place great value on relationships. King David was commended as being "a man after God's own heart." You can be, also.

   Relationship is always more important than any issue being discussed. Do not determine to win a conflict at the expense of damaging fellowship with that person.

2. *Change your perspective!*

   Value the other person, their feelings, their situation and their ideas. Be open to accepting the other person's situations or ideas!

   When the adulteress was brought to Jesus, and Jesus was expected to condemn her, Jesus resolved a conflict between the woman needing forgiveness and her accusers. He successfully resolved the conflict by changing her accusers' perspective. He made them realize that they also had faults in their lives.

   Anyway, your opinion or solution is not always the best, or the only good solution. That is known as "opinion idolatry", and it has no place in successful families and relationships.

3. *Uphold Respect for the other person.*

   A key to successful conflict resolution is that both parties maintain respect for each other. During conflict, often strife intensifies as we lose respect for the other person, and our hearts get harder toward each other. Never let a conflict damage the respect you have for the other person.

4. *Never discuss a conflict when emotions are high.*

   Calm down first. Remember that communication is 25% words and 75% tone of voice --- what is really heard is not so much what you say, but how you say it. James 1: 19 says, "Everyone should be quick to listen, slow to speak and slow to become angry."

5. *Prayer is a necessary ingredient.*

   Retreat from attacking and blaming your spouse, and advance in prayer and in using God's Word against the devil.

As you pray over the conflict, you will start to see the conflict in a different light. Pastor Dino Rizzo (Sr. Pastor at Healing Place Church, Baton Rouge, LA) says, "My whole world looks totally different when I am on my knees in prayer. Prayer gives me a different perspective." Those things that seem so important to us in the natural look very different when we spend time in the presence of God.

Pray! Pray together and for each other. Pray before you discuss the issue. Pray - asking God to show you a reasonable compromise for each issue.

If you disagree with a decision your spouse has made, do not get angry, show disrespect or put them down. We all make mistakes. Love them anyway. Do not let the decision drive a wedge between you and your spouse.

6. *Agreeing to disagree!*

There are times when, after extended discussions on an issue, no adequate resolution is found. At that point, we just need to "agree to disagree", and let it go. Let go, for the sake of your relationship.

Acts of Resolving Conflicts:

1. *Initiate a meeting to discuss the conflict.*

The conflict will not resolve itself. Matthew 18: 15 reads, "If your brother sins against you, go and show him his fault, just between the two of you." If he listens to you, you have won your brother over."

2. *Involve a mediator, if necessary.*

Often, a 3rd party who is not involved in the situation can see the conflict in a different light, and propose a reasonable solution.

3. *Give to the one who asks you --- Do not resist!*

Matthew 5: 39-42 "But I tell you, do not resist an evil person. If someone strikes you on the right cheek, turn to him the other also. And if someone wants to sue you and take your tunic, let him have your cloak as well. If someone forces you to go one mile, go with him two miles. *Give to the one who asks you, and do not turn away from the one who wants to borrow from you.*"

Please understand that Jesus is not interested in having disciples who are weak and afraid. He is interested in His disciples valuing people and expressing love.

Philippians 2: 3-4 says, "Do nothing out of selfish ambition or vain conceit, but in humility consider others better than yourselves. Each of you should look not only to your own interests, but also to the interests of others."

Giving will maintain and enhance relationships!

4. *Regain respect!*

Have you already lost respect for your spouse or stepchild? Pray through! Ask God to re-establish respect in your heart. Make a list of the good qualities your spouse or stepchild has.

5. *Admit when you are wrong!*

6. *Apology is mandatory --- saying you are sorry when you have acted poorly!*

7. *Forgive --- for any harsh words spoken or offensive action!*

8. *Affirm your love for your spouse & children!*

9. *Pray!*

Moe & Paige Becnel

Appendix C   Suggested Drama Scripts

Drama 1   Your Rules – My Rules
By Shanna Forrestall

Tommy	*Is in the living room, reading a newspaper.*
Maria	***Is agitated, comes into the room and interrupts him. Tommy***
Tommy	Yeah, honey… *barely looks up.*
Maria	**I need to talk to you.**
Tommy	Yeah… *still doesn't look up*
Maria	**Now!**
Tommy	*Looks up when he realizes she's agitated.* OK, what's up?
Maria	**It's Thomas. He has been riding his bike too far down the street again.**
Tommy	It's ok. I told you, I've taught him how to watch for cars, and he's a pretty careful kid.
Maria	**CAREFUL KID? That's an oxymoron. Kids are not careful.**
Tommy	Thomas is.
Maria	**Tommy …he's still a boy. You can't treat him like he's a full-grown man. He could get hurt.**
Tommy	Look, Maria, I know you're only worrying about him because you care, but he can handle it… he has been riding alone since he started riding his bike…
Maria	**Tommy, that's not good enough. He is partly my responsibility now and I need to feel like he's being looked after.**
Tommy	*Getting agitated, feels like she is questioning his concern for the child.* Well, he is…!
Maria	**Look, if we are ever going to become a family we have to come together on these things…**
Tommy	*Cuts her off…* What? Come to your opinion?!?
Maria	***Cuts him short,*** **That's not what I meant.**
Tommy	Well, what do you mean?
Maria	**I don't know, it's just that… well, it's too confusing when we don't agree on things…**
Tommy	Like…
Maria	**Well, it's almost like we have two sets of rules, your rules and my rules.**
Tommy	So.
Maria	**Well, how are they supposed to obey if we don't even agree?**
Tommy	Good point. *Thinks about it.* Maybe we need to work on consolidating.
Maria	**Consolidating? How? *She calms down as she realizes he is trying to help her come up with a solution.***
Tommy	I'm not sure. How about one set of rules? We'll write them together.
Maria	**You think that will work? *She is unsure.***
Tommy	It could.
Maria	**So…no more your rules and my rules…**
Tommy	That's right, from now on, it could be Our Rules. *Puts out his hand* Deal?
Maria	***She grabs his hand.* That's right – Our Rules.**
Tommy	*Thinks for a second…* OK, I've got it - Rule No. 1 – only adults over 30 get to eat the Chocolate Macadamia Nut Ice Cream
Maria	**Seconded by the mom in charge. *She nods agreeing with him.***
Tommy	Race you to the fridge.
Maria	***Points to the corner.* Look! *She distracts him and takes off running, he follows off-stage.***

Drama 2   You're Not My Father
By Shanna Forrestall

Samantha	Comes in the door, obviously in a hurry to get some answers.
Frank	*Is sitting at the kitchen table working on bills. Looks up when she enters.*
Frank	**Hi Samantha** *(goes back to his work)*
Samantha	*Starts to walk by without answering and then stops to ask him a question.* Hi Frank, where's my mother?
Frank	**Your mother and my wife is at the mall…**
Samantha	Ugh, *disappointed, because she wanted to talk to her…*
Frank	**She should be back soon.**
Samantha	From the mall? Yeah, right. Did she take her cell-phone?
Frank	**No, she forgot it again, I saw it in the bathroom.**
Samantha	*Obviously getting agitated. Looks at her watch and sits at the table, begins digging in her purse.*
Frank	**So, got any plans for tonight?**
Samantha	What's it to you?
Frank	**Just wondering.**
Samantha	Oh, so you can shut them down, like you did last weekend?
Frank	**I explained that.**
Samantha	Yeah, you explained it… "I just don't feel you should go…", yeah, good explanation…
Frank	**I'm just trying to look out for your best interest.**
Samantha	That's not your job.
Frank	**Sure it is.**
Samantha	No, it's not.
Frank	**Then whose is it?**
Samantha	My mom's!
Frank	**You don't think she could use some help sometimes?**
Samantha	Who do you think you are? Just because you married her, does not mean we are destined to have some kind of a close relationship.
Frank	**I was hoping we would… some day.**
Samantha	Give it up! (*Stands up to leave, clearly agitated.)*
Frank	*Watches her stand, he is obviously hurt and wants to make things right.* **So, what do you have planned for the weekend?**
Samantha	Why?
Frank	**I was just wondering**
Samantha	Stop wondering. You're NOT my father. *She walks out of the room*
Frank	*Hangs his head*

ORDER FORM

To order more Books and Workbooks for friends, neighbors, or co-workers:

GOD BREATHES ON BLENDED FAMILIES
ISBN: 0-9678680-0-9   Retail: $9.00 X Quantity_____ = Total_____

GOD BREATHES ON BLENDED FAMILIES WORKBOOK
ISBN: 0-9678680-1-7   Retail: $12.95 X Quantity_____ = Total_____

Please complete this order form and mail to:
Healing Place Church
19202 Highland Road   or call HPC at 1-225-753-2273
Baton Rouge, LA 70809   or order on-line at www.healingplacechurch.org/products

START YOUR OWN BLENDING A FAMILY SUPPORT GROUP!

CALL FOR QUANTITY DISCOUNTS!

ORDER FORM

To order more Books and Workbooks for friends, neighbors, or co-workers:

GOD BREATHES ON BLENDED FAMILIES
ISBN: 0-9678680-0-9   Retail: $9.00 X Quantity_____ = Total_____

GOD BREATHES ON BLENDED FAMILIES WORKBOOK
ISBN: 0-9678680-1-7   Retail: $12.95 X Quantity_____ = Total_____

Please complete this order form and mail to:
Healing Place Church   or call HPC at 1-225-753-2273
19202 Highland Road
Baton Rouge, LA 70809   or order on-line at www.healingplacechurch.org/products

START YOUR OWN BLENDING A FAMILY SUPPORT GROUP!

CALL FOR QUANTITY DISCOUNTS!